NO ONE HAS TO DIE! A True Story plus, The Legal, Medical, Lifesaving, and Enjoyable Aspects of High Technology

By: Tina Schaneville

Tina Schaneville

P.O. Box 482

Chalmette, La. 70044

1-706-360-3410

Cyber4us1@gmail.com

Library of Congress ISBN #

Abstract

Thesis: New computer technology can affect society wonderfully, promote safety, prohibit accidents, and facilitate life in many ways. If mandatory laws are established in information technology in different areas of society, the world will be a safer, better, happier, and healthier place to live.

This paper describes different types of new technology that can help society in wonderful ways. Some problems that exist in society are drunk driving, illegal drug addiction, identity theft, and computer hacking for monetary gain. This paper examines new technologies available to prohibit terrible actions from occurring. Furthermore, this paper examines the lighter side of computer technology purely for enjoyment, and making life easier on people. Therefore, new computer technology is mandatory to prohibit accidents, promote safety, protect against theft of any kind, and make life easier for society as a whole.

Table of Contents

Dedication on 03-17-2010

I dedicate this book to my children: Charie Billiot, Chrissie Billiot, and Brian Lafontaine (in alphabetical order). I love all my children dearly!

Charie Ann Billiot was a beautiful, friendly, nice, and intelligent young lady. She was almost always on the Academic Honor Roll. She studied gymnastics and dancing in her spare time. Charie became a cheerleader for her high school called Chalmette High School. She was in the math honors club. She was the best daughter any mother could have! She even was thoughtful and remembered her biological mother, Tina, on Mother's Day by making her own mother's day cards. She was extremely talented in many areas of life. Charie gave her mother, Tina, plenty of hugs and kisses on the cheek. Tina loves and misses her daughter extremely much! Tina hopes to see her again in Heaven.

Brian James Lafontaine was a handsome, friendly, nice, and intelligent young man. He was a good student. He played football when he was a young boy. He was popular and would try to help anyone who needed help. Brian was a good son to his biological mother, Tina. He, too, would make Mother's Day cards to give to Tina. He had a good relationship with his mother. Tina loves and misses, Brian. Tina hopes to see him again in Heaven.

Chrissie Ann Billiot is a beautiful, friendly, nice, and intelligent young lady. She is almost always on the Academic Honor Roll. She has studied gymnastics and dancing in her spare time with her sister, Charie. Chrissie has become a cheerleader for her high school. She is the best daughter any mother could have! She even is thoughtful and remembers her biological mother, Tina, on Mother's Day by making her own mother's day cards. She is extremely talented in many areas of life. Chrissie gives her mother, Tina, plenty of hugs and kisses on the cheek. Tina loves her daughter extremely much! Tina sees Chrissie on a regular basis when she has time off from college. Chrissie Ann Billiot is the only surviving child of Tina Schaneville because she was wearing a seat belt on the day of the August 21st, 2005 automobile accident.

- Due to formatting reasons and printing costs, the photos of all the children are located in the back of this book.

Preface, A True Story

I dedicate this book to my children: Charie Billiot, Chrissie Billiot, and Brian Lafontaine (in alphabetical order). I love all my children dearly! I use the present tense even though two (Charie and Brian) are deceased because their souls exist eternally in Heaven. I tried my best as a parent even though I had many obstacles to overcome emotionally and some physically. I have tried my best to instill good values in all my children, and to be a good role model in terms of being a good citizen. I spent quality time with them at the park outdoors, playing baseball with plastic equipment; reading Dr. Seuss books; watching rented Blockbuster movies, and eating our favorite, healthy, and nutritious foods.

When people are young, people make mistakes in life. It is my wish to try to prevent any mistakes and future accidents by providing some important information in this book for parents, teachers, the government, and society as a whole. We, as a society must learn, and try to prevent dangerous events from happening. I lost my two teenagers in a traffic accident due to drunk driving. I was not involved in the accident at all. I do not drink alcohol. I do not take any illegal drugs. I do not smoke cigarettes. I have tried my best to instill good values in all my children. However, I must endure sadness for the rest of my natural born life. Therefore, I have provided much valuable information in this book to try to prevent dangerous and fatal accidents from happening. I wish everyone good luck and safety in life. May the Creator of the Universe bless people who try to choose the correct path in life, and have good intentions!

On August 21st, 2005, a group of teenagers from two high schools embarked on a journey. They went to go tubing at a commercial recreation place on the Boguechitto River in Bogalusa, Louisiana. The teenagers were to spend the day at a commercial tubing place in Bogalusa, Louisiana. They stopped at the Lose Puckie (names are changed for legal purposes) Grocery store in Chalmette, Louisiana to purchase more beverages. There were many witnesses who stated that beer and alcohol was sold to underage teenagers. The grocery store is negligent for not taking age identification cards of minors and for the illegal sale of alcohol to minors. A few of the local groceries and quick stops in Chalmette, Louisiana were negligent for the illegal sale of alcohol to minors. There were many witnesses of friends of the wonderful teenagers that died who corroborated the illegal sale of alcohol to minors. Some teenagers did not want to get into trouble, and lied about the incident. However, the truth came out eventually, and the Creator of the Universe does not like liars! Not only were the grocery stores and quick stops negligent, but the tubing place allowed the teenagers to drink all day long while coming down the Boguechitto River.

At approximately 4 p.m., the teenagers finished their float down the Boguechitto River in Bogalusa, Louisiana. Many decided that they needed to get back home to their responsibilities of work, chores, and other duties to be done. Most probably, Brian was going to try to go to work that evening. However, he was too drunk to drive. The people at the tubing place even told him how to dodge the police roadblock by going down a winding road with many large trees. One of the teenagers tried to stop him from driving by trying to take his car keys away. However, Brian was too muscular from working out and too drunk to listen to his friend. His friend is a hero for trying to take the car keys away. Anyone could have been a hero; had they just called the police to try to stop what was happening with a potential for danger. The danger is a drunken teenager with no sober designated driver who drives home drunk.

On August 21, 2005, Tina was notified at about 2 hours later than the accident. She remembers it was dark outside when someone told her to go to the Lakeland Hospital in Covington, Louisiana. She drove there hoping all of her children were alright. Then, she receives a call from Chuck Billiot, the teenagers' biological father of Charie and Chrissie Billiot. All she could hear in the background were people crying and Chuck saying, "Oh, no! Not Charie!".

Tina finally arrived at the Lakeland Memorial Hospital in Covington, Louisiana. Everyone was crying and screaming. It was difficult to find out what was happening. Finally, someone told me that Brian Lafontaine was taken by ambulance to Charity Hospital because there were more workers there with plenty of medical equipment. Tina did not know what to do. Her three children were separated into three different hospitals. Charie Ann Billiot was at the Bogalusa Hospital. Chrissie Ann Billiot was at the Lakeland Hospital. Brian Lafontaine was being taken to the Charity Hospital due to not having enough doctors on call at the Lakeland Hospital. It was a total nightmare! Tina could not believe what was happening!

Tina Schaneville did not know anything about the tubing trip. She lived at another residence. She had been divorced for many years. However, Tina Schaneville maintained her rightful visitation with all of her three teenagers. She spent quality time with them playing sports at the local park; reading Dr. Seuss books; watching Blockbuster movies, and eating healthy, delicious, and nutritious food. Tina had a wonderful relationship with all of her teenagers up until the day that they died. They all visited on a regular basis. Tina feels a major loss of love!

Tina was told by the doctor to stay at Lakeland Hospital because Chrissie was going to be the only offspring to survive this terrible, fatal vehicular accident. Tina stayed up non-stop for approximately 2 and half days at Chrissie Ann Billiot's side. Tina held Chrissie's hand and spoke to her sometimes. When the danger passed after Chrissie's head operation, Tina drove home to shower and sleep.

A week later, the hurricane Katrina struck Chalmette, Louisiana. Many southern cities in south Louisiana were extremely flooded. It looked like a lake. Tina wanted to dress Charie up in a lovely purple print dress for the wake. Tina wanted to say goodbye to Charie Ann Billiot and Brian James Lafontaine. However, they were left at the morgue. Everyone was ordered to evacuate Chalmette, Louisiana. Tina did not get to say goodbye to her precious children. The only surviving teenager of Tina Schaneville is Chrissie Ann Billiot who was wearing a seatbelt. The others were not.

The following people were involved in this terrible tragedy:

1.) All of the teenagers were good teenagers on the honor roll who would help anyone that needed help in anything.

2.) All of the attorneys on the plaintiff side for the families of the deceased teenagers and severely injured teenagers are dedicated, honest lawyers.

3.) All of the parents on the plaintiff side for all of the deceased teenagers and severely injured teenagers are good, respectable citizens of society.

Tina is writing this book to try to prevent other teenagers from dying in a terrible, fatal accident. Teenagers need the following: Proper and regular counseling; instilling of values and morals; attending church; showing photos of wrecked vehicles and incapacitated people; regular blood tests to test for alcohol and illegal drugs should be administered once monthly. If the teenager is on any type of alcohol or drugs, then the teenager must be counseled regularly while in incarceration because parents cannot keep teenagers at home themselves. Contact the state where the person lives to find appropriate rehabilitation hospitals. Many people do not realize how enormous the alcohol and illegal drug problem truly is. DO NOT LET THE DRUG OR ALCOHOL PUSHER GET YOUR PRECIOUS TEENAGERS!!!! FIGHT THE DEVIL AND EVIL!!!!

About the Book, Author, & Her Career

02-25-2012

Tina's book consists of scholarly articles with proper references, and a statistics test with a math problem to prove something. She is currently tutoring young adults so that they can obtain their GED. It is a good deed. This is excellent for her resume as teaching experience. Tina is near the end of her program in education for her Ph.D. doctorate degree currently in the area of Information Technology.

Tina Schaneville

P.O. Box 482

Chalmette, La.   70044

1-706-360-3410

Cyber4us1@gmail.com

Drunken Driving

Wells-Parker (2004) states that alcohol related crime offenders driving under the influence [DUI], and underage drinking) should be sentenced to participate in some form of treatment for alcohol problems. This can be rehabilitative treatment designed for excessive alcoholic drinking and its harmful consequences. Court-mandated treatment is a main way for many people to receive the alcoholic treatment (Weisner et al. 2002, p. 42). The words mandated treatment and coercion are usually used (Farabee et al. 1998). Mandated treatment is "legal consequences if individuals refuse to comply "(Polcin and Greenfield 2003, p. 650). Jail time and house arrest are excellent punishments; which gives the alcoholic time to think about trying to change for the better (Cavaiola & Wuth, 2002). DUI (Driving Under Influence) offenders can participate in different alcoholism treatment programs (Cavaiola & Wuth, 2002; Wells-Parker et al., 1995). Alcoholics Anonymous (AA) is a group that strives to reduce drinking and driving with the following: Education programs and testimonials by injured survivors or families of victims killed in alcohol-related crashes (i.e., victim impact panels). Mandated interventions often include supervised probation and computer aided devices worn on the leg for home arrest monitoring as well. Alcoholics Anonymous can provide supportive contact that could reduce driving while impaired (Wells-Parker, 2004).

Wells-Parker (2004) acknowledges two sanctions that prevent offenders from drinking under the influence of alcohol are license revocation and alcohol ignition interlocks, which require the driver to pass an alcohol breath test before starting a car. In a study (Mann et al. 1994), offenders who received treatment and sanctions had lower fatality rates after some years than members who did not receive counseling and sanctions. New technological devices, such as alcohol ignition interlocks and electronic monitoring devices, which allow home detention and remote BAC (Blood Alcohol Content) monitoring (Voas, 2004),can be effectively used to reduce DUI (Driving Under Influence). Court mandated use of computer devices to reduce DUI must be initiated as common practice worldwide. Technological monitoring would allow courts to handle effectively alcoholic offenders. Research shows that the breath test results recorded on interlocks are particularly effective in reducing DUI (Marques et al. 2003). Therefore, computer devices must be court mandated treatment to effectively treat and prevent DUI; along with counseling to show fatality and mortality percentages as a result of DUI (Voas, 2004) (Wells-Parker, 2004).

Wells-Parker (2004) gives the fact that a computer device that measures an individual's blood alcohol content (BAC) is called an alcohol ignition interlock. It is part of the ignition system of a vehicle and is designed to prevent the vehicle from being started if the driver's BAC exceeds the legal limit. Interlocks provide safety for drivers to avoid drunken driving (Weinrath, 1997). In addition, the device allows drivers to re-enter the licensing system legally, with insurance rather than permitting offenders to continue to drive unlicensed without supervision (Beirness & Simpson, 1991). Ignition interlock serves as a constant reminder to the driver of possible difficulties that can result from drunk driving. Interlocks also offer many offenders the opportunity to drive; whereas many offenders may not have had have the opportunity of convenient transportation (Beirness & Simpson, 1991) (Wells-Parker, 2004).

Wells-Parker (2004) gives knowledge from Morse and Elliot (1992) in Ohio reported that when interlocks were installed, DUI rates were lower (65% reduction) than for offenders given only license suspension. Furthermore, Popkin et al. (1992) in North Carolina and Jones (1992) in Oregon performed interlock trials and reported much lower re-arrest rates for interlock participants. Beck et al. (1997) in Maryland conducted an interlock trial and reported a 65% reduction in DUI. Finally, Weinrath (1997) examined the combination of interlocks with a support program, which showed wonderful results in safety for prevention of injuries and fatalities in collisions (Wells-Parker, 2004).

Wells-Parker (2004) declares that many interlock studies have reported that after the interlock was removed

from the vehicle many drivers returned to DUI (Beck et al. 1997; Jones 1992; Morse and Elliot 1992;

Popkin et al. 1992; Was et al. 1999). The interlock device loses any beneficial effect upon removal (Weinrath, 1997). Studies demonstrate that interlocks are a feasible countermeasure. Participants stated that using the device reminded them of blood alcohol content. Most believe that the device is a terrific sentencing option rather than traditional legal sanctions (Coxon & Earl 1998; Spencer, 2000) (Wells-Parker, 2004).

Gordon (2010) states that Claes Tingvall, President of the Highway Traffic Safety Department in Sweden; declares that the auto industry's main concern is car safety. Volvo, Saab, Nissan and Mercedes-Benz have been studying sleep-deprived drivers in simulated driving scenarios to ascertain the most effective way to alert drowsy drivers. Volvo has made the 'Driver Alert' system. If the car notices that the driver is drowsing, the vehicle makes a loud noise alarm, and an icon showing a cup of coffee, which flashes on the dashboard (Edmunds, 2010). Saab has created the 'Driver Attention Warning System' that uses a voice alarm: "You are tired, you are dangerously tired! Stop as soon as it is safe to do so!" In addition to the voice alarm, the driver's seat vibrates to help alert the driver (Forbes, 2007). Saab's utilizes facial recognition software to ascertain if the driver is drowsy. Night vision cameras pointed on the face analyze the eyes (Forbes, 2007) (Gordon, 2010).

Electronic Monitoring with a Computer Ankle Bracelet

Florida Department of Corrections (FDOC, 2003) states that this study shows the effectiveness of electronic monitoring (EM) for criminal offenders monitored in the state of Florida, United States of America. Using data on 75,661 offenders placed on home confinement in Florida from 1998 to 2002, evidence shows that both radio frequency and global positioning system monitoring greatly reduce the likelihood of reoffending. Policy Implications:

The results presented here suggest that electronic monitoring of offenders is an effective public safety alternative to prison. Additional implications of this research include which monitoring device will be the most cost-effective and efficient (FDOC, 2003).

FDOC (2003) gives a report from Austin et al. (2003) that from 1980 to the year 2000, prisoners rose to a level of more than tripled. The widely publicized rape and murder of nine-year-old Jessica Lunsford in 2005, by a registered sex offender, created legislation in Florida that requires sex offenders to wear satellite tracking devices (global positioning system, or GPS, monitoring) for the rest of their lives when they leave prison. This study shows the effectiveness of electronic monitoring (EM) for serious offenders. In 1983, Florida became the first state to legislate and implement a home confinement program (FDOC, 2003). As the program developed, different offenders required different amounts of supervision. Since 1987, with legislative approval, the FDOC implemented RF monitoring. In 1998, the use of electronic monitoring was expanded to include GPS monitoring for those offenders of higher risk to the public with an even higher level of surveillance (FDOC, 2003).

FDOC (2003) declares that the GPS (Global Positioning System) system two-way communication with the victim or the offender, location mapping, immediate tamper notification, remote laptop tracking with a wireless modem for constant communication with the monitoring center are effective. Offenders are supposed to be told that violations are tracked in real time 24 hours a day (FDOC, 2003).

FDOC (2003) conducts the Empirical Test for electronic monitoring:

The following parameters are taken into account for this test:

1.) Socio-demographic Characteristics of the Offender: Age, race, and sex are included. Marital status is not included.

2.) Current Primary Offense: (1) murder/ manslaughter, (2) sex offenses, (3) robbery, (4) other violent/personal offenses, (5) burglary, (6) theft, (7) drug offenses, (8) weapons offenses, and (9) "other" offenses.

3.) Current Sentence.

4.) Conditions of Supervision: participation in a treatment program (domestic violence, psychological, drug, and/or sex offender treatment); participation in an educational program, regular drug testing, and/ or the completion of public service hours

FDOC (2003).

FDOC (2003) emphatically declares that criminal offenders on electronic monitoring have less of a chance to be revoked for a technical violation. In fact, offenders on global positioning system (GPS) monitoring are 90.2% less likely than offenders without electronic monitoring (EM). The z score = 2.962, which supports hypothesis that offenders on the more intense form of electronic surveillance can get caught violating the conditions of their home confinement sentence (FDOC, 2003).

FDOC (2003) gives proof that electronic monitoring was effective in reducing reoffending. The use of GPS monitoring had virtually the same inhibiting effect on revocations and absconding for violent, and drug offenders. Electronic monitoring works well for all kinds of serious offenders (violent, property, or drug). The decision about which offenders should be electronically monitored will need to be based on the primary offense. Electronic monitoring can be used to produce more refined forms of control for offenders that are used in a manner that produces maximum desired results. Technology makes it possible to control criminals better. Consequently, systematic research is fundamental if society is to maximize the potentials associated with these technologies in a rapidly changing culture (Garland, 2004) (FDOC, 2003).

Identity Theft

Busch (2006) states that for more than a hundred years, investigators have utilized fingerprints to identify criminals at the crime scene. Computers facilitate the criminal identification process. The process is called the Automated Fingerprint Identification System (AFIS) in the United States and some other countries. AFIS only takes a few seconds to complete (Busch, 2006).

Busch (2006) declares that there are different sectors of society that use biometric identification. Biometric identification identifies a person by using fingerprints, hands, iris, or retina of the eyes. Biometric identification can also use voice recognition, or code of letters and numbers (Busch, 2006).

Busch (2006) states that the US border office obtains the prints of both index fingers, and a digital portrait photo. This security action is used to fight terrorism and to monitor residence permits. This was initiated in 2004, and within a few months the system was a success to spot potential criminals (Busch, 2006).

Busch (2006) gives information about the Epass, which is for identification when entering European countries. The Epass contains a digitized photo of a person and fingerprints. A 3D photo is better for identification and security. This type of passport now contains biometric identification on the passport. The Epass is a better way to identify individuals especially when travelling (Busch, 2006).

Busch (2006) explicitly states the advantage of biometric authentication is that it eliminates some risk of information, passwords, or chip cards) from being stolen. Biometric systems will enable access to secure facilities such as the following: nuclear power stations or emergency service control centers. Moreover, a digital citizen card may also include e-government, e-banking or e-business access. Computer hacker access and security demands may initiate further progress in biometric research (Busch, 2006).

Computer Hacking

Thompson (2008) declares that new types of worms can leave backdoors open for a bot's entrance. The bot, then builds a "botnet" which is a network of computers to destroy personal data, and to hurt websites in many ways. Botnets usually are used to commit computer hacking for fraud, identity theft and online extortion (Thompson, 2008).

Thompson (2008) states that banks in the United Kingdom estimated that malware losses in 2006 were £33.5 million ($62 million). Malware losses are increasing as time elapses. The United States paid $7.8 billion as a result of malware. Individual users are typical victims. A 2005 report commissioned by the Australian government revealed that many users do not use current antivirus software and firewalls. In the US, many users prevent computer viruses and spyware by installing anti-virus software on the computer. Anti-virus software downloads virus definitions so that it can recognize and destroy any computer viruses, worms, or Trojan Horses (Thompson, 2008).

Thompson (2008) declares protecting networks is mandatory and anticipating threats is much better than removing threats. Malware attacks mobile devices, also. In the report, 'Malware: A security Threat to the Internet Economy', the OECD states that governments, the private sector, the technical and the civil communities band together to form

an "Anti-Malware Partnership" to find ways to reduce malware, and establish codes of practice.

Malware is no longer a prank but a form of cybercrime (Thompson, 2008).

Artificial Intelligence and Androids

Brown (2009) declares that the International Federation of Robotics predicts that by the end of 2011 the world's population of service robots could exceed more than 17 million robots. The Japanese Robotics Association predicts a $15 billion market for service robots by 2015. Some service robots will have just enough intelligence to do basic jobs. One robot is Roomba, a vacuum cleaner. Roomba cleans in spiral shapes and follows walls. When it bumps into furniture, it changes course. Roomba cleans slowly. Many janitors may have to find alternate work because Roomba's sales peaked at 3.3 million at the end of 2007. Another cleaning robot is iRobot, which scrubs floors, cleans pools, sweeps home shops, and ejects leaves from gutters. Robotic lawn mowers totaled 110,000 in sales at the end of 2007 (Brown, 2009).

Brown (2009) declares that other types of robots sell well, also. Lego Entertainment robots teach children basics. Sony Corporation's $2,500 Aibo robotic dog can see, recognize commands, and learn new tricks. Two million entertainment robots sold for a total of $2 billion through 2007. The service robots for professional usage are smarter and more sophisticated. The International Federation of Robotics estimates that 49,000 robots were sold in 2007 for approximately $ 7.8 billion. Service robots for defense, rescue, and security sold 12,000

robots. Irobot sold more than 2,000 PackBot robots for war purposes. England's QinetiQ Group manufactures

Talon, a robot that can run in war. Field robots, such as milking machines acquired 20 percent of the market in

the International Federation of Robotics' survey. Skywash from Germany's Putzmeister Werke generates

motion programs from CAD (Computer Aided Diagram) diagrams and cleans aircraft. Aquatic underwater

robots for offshore oil pipelines make up 12 percent of the market, construction (9 percent), medical robots (9

percent), and mobile robot platforms (7.4 percent). Logistic and inspection systems held 5.6 percent of the

market. The market for handicap robots is growing for disabled, handicapped persons, and robotic prostheses

especially due to injured soldiers missing body parts. Therefore, the robot world population is increasing

(Brown, 2009).

Advanced Female Android Created By Le Trung in Canada in 2007

Trung (2010) discusses Project Aiko which describes the creation of a Yumecom (TM)

Aiko (Yumecom = Dream Computer Robot). The main goal of Le Trung was to create Aiko to help

elderly and disabled people to do simple tasks. Simple tasks include making tea and coffee;

stating the weather; reading, or reminding them to do important tasks. The android, Aiko, can be

utilized in the home, office or public places (Trung, 2010).

Trung (2010) declares that Aiko was created in his home basement. His funding was his

finances, which included credit card loans, and his savings. On April 12th, 2010, Aiko is not fully

functioning because she needs to be able to walk and do chores. Mr. Le Trung states that people can donate any amount of monetary funding. The donations will go towards

new motors, sensors and main boards to design Aiko's body (Trung, 2010).

Trung (2010) created Aiko to react to physical stimuli and mimic pain. This is the first

Android to have this reaction. This technology could be applied to disabled people who need

computer assistance for movement of arms, legs, or other body parts. Mr. Le Trung initiated

creating Aiko on August 15, 2007. Approximately a month and a half later, Aiko version 1

was finished. Aiko made her debut at the Hobby Show on November 2007 at the Toronto

International Center. Another appearance was made at the Ontario Science Center a week later.

Aiko is currently bilingual. The female android can speak English and Japanese. However,

that will change to include more languages when better software and hardware is purchased

(Trung, 2010).

Le Trung (2010) states Aiko's Height and Measurements are the following:

Height 152cm Bust: 82cm Waist: 57cm Hip: 84cm
Height 5 ft Bust: 32" Waist: 23" Hip: 33"   (Trung, 2010).

To contact Le Trung as of April 12th, 2010:

Website: http://www.projectaiko.com/contact.html

By: Tina Schaneville

Email: info@projectaiko.com

Address: Le Trung

        Brampton, Ontario

        Canada

Phone: 1718-395-752

Robots are Beneficial to Society

Robots and Treadmill Training

Krassioukov et Al. (2011) state the purpose of the study is to show a new way to BWSTT with forces to resist leg movements during gait. The application of force that can resist leg flexes during the swing can be beneficial to strengthen motors. The level of perceived exertion and cardiovascular tolerance during training is measured. The walking was performed over ground (Krassioukov et Al., 2011).

Krassioukov et Al. (2011) state that the participant is a 43-year-old man (height=180 cm, weight=77 kg). He suffered a traumatic SCI due to a T12 burst fracture following a fall. This occurred 2 years prior to the study. He was an independent person. He used a wheelchair. However, he was able to stand and walk indoors for short periods during the day (Krassioukov et Al., 2011).

Krassioukov et Al. (2011) discuss BWSTT with resistance training using Lokomat-applied forces. The results show that this is a beneficial approach to improving functional ambulation in people with chronic motor-incomplete SCI. The participant showed improvement in walking, stair climbing, and walking up a ramp. The participant improved cardiovascularly. He even developed confidence. In summary, this study has shown success in using a new BWSTT strategy using robot-applied resistance against leg movements (Krassioukov et Al., 2011).

Robots Perform Heart Microsurgery

Salisbury (1998) announces an important milestone in medical history was achieved in May 1998. Surgeons first started using robots in heart surgery. The operation consisted of repairing a heart valve. This marks the first time ever that robots were used to assist in the heart operation. The shrinking robots and growing processors were used to achieve a minimal invasive heart surgery. The patient's defective valve was cut and reconstructed. The operation was remarkable because robots were used. There have been heart valve operations before this one. However, this one is special because it utilized minute robots to achieve a minimally invasive technique. It was so small of body invasion that the surgeon's hands never entered the patient's body. The surgeon was not even near the patient by operating table. The operation was a surgical system that controlled instruments inserted through small incisions less than one centimeter (0.4 inch) long. The cardiologist controlled the system 20 feet away. He utilized telerobotic arms in the patient's body, and viewed three-dimensional images on a monitor screen. A minute camera was inserted into the patient's body to be able to see inside the body. The cardiologist performed the operation with a high level of precision that is impossible without the use of robots (Salisbury, 1998).

Salisbury (1998) declares that this operation was first performed in Paris, France and in Leipzig, Germany using a tele-robotic system developed by Intuitive Surgical Inc. of Mountain View, California, United States of America. In June, a "closed chest" video-scoped coronary artery bypass graft was achieved. Many heart patients will recover faster due to the minimal invasive surgery. Therefore, cardiac heart surgery patients will receive the benefits of a truly minimal invasive operation (Salisbury, 1998).

Robots Perform Neurological Surgery

Shen, Shen, and Gu (2007) declare that head injury is a significant cause of death. Lack of monetary funds and geographical position can mean the difference between life and death. However, tele-robotic neurosurgery is the answer to this terrible problem. In this application, the remote perforator on a robot arm drills a hole on the skull of person to relieve pressure from head trauma and life threatening conditions. The tele-robotic neurosurgical system includes the perforator, the robot arm, the camera, the optical tracking system, and the force feedback joystick. The CT or MRI diagnostic images are used for future surgery (Shen, Shen, & Gu, 2007).

Shen, Shen, and Gu (2007) emphasize that the purpose of this article is to consider surgical robotics, with a focus on technology and design issues for remote-mode operation assistance. The investigation leads to the definition of the technical characteristics of a co-robotic positioning device (CRPD). Robotics is a multidisciplinary technology, developed to fulfill tasks with no direct human intervention. The medical application of robots is one of the most promising developments in robotic industry. Robots are performing tasks such as delivering specimens, patient records, diagnosis, treatment, and even surgery. Telesurgery means that surgeons operate on the patient remotely. The most popular medical robotic application is minimally invasive surgery (MIS, surgery conducted with a robot for less risk of infection and faster recovery with less pain and no blood loss). The Da Vinci Surgical System is a MIS technology (Shen, Shen, & Gu, 2007).

Robots Perform Minimally Invasive Surgery

Michelini and Razzoli (2008) report that minimally invasive surgery is used on many other body parts. One in particular is the gall bladder. It is far more economical with minimally invasive surgery. Today, many people receive surgery this way in order to heal faster and have less pain. This procedure enables the operation to be more natural with less invasion and internal damage. Engineers still strive to invent a better operation procedure to be better than the minimally invasive technique (Michelini & Razzoli, 2008).

Michelini and Razzoli (2008) state that the Defense Advanced Research Projects Administration, or DARPA, in Arlington, Va. utilized the Internet to have telesurgery to save soldiers on the battlefield when time is of the essence in saving a life. Later, when stabilized the soldiers would be moved to a safe hospital close by the scene of the injury. Using telesurgery via satellite, the military's best trauma surgeons could perform surgery in remote locations. In1995, using technology developed at SRI, IBM, and the Massachusetts Institute of Technology, Intuitive's engineers developed robotic arms and instruments for difficult reconstructive surgery through one-centimeter incisions. A proprietary 3-D video camera and stereo viewer was developed to provide a view inside a patient's body. With a magnified surgical site, a coronary artery (a few millimeters in diameter) can be enlarged on screen to appear as large as a garden hose. Every move the surgeon makes is precise with the aid of surgical electromechanical instruments inside the patient's body. The computer system controls the robot arms and provides feedback. During a procedure, the Intuitive system monitors continuously, and alerts the surgeon of any problems. A wide variety of tools has been developed for needle grasping, cutting, cautery, and clip application. Kenneth Salisbury, Jr., is a scientific adviser with Intuitive Surgical Inc. in Mountain View, Calif. He works at the Massachusetts Institute of Technology in Cambridge (Michelini & Razzoli, 2008).

Robots Rehabilitate People

Godfrey (2010) states that robotic walking machines help to rehabilitate people. A rehabilitation machine such as the MIT robot "MANUS" is for stroke victims. The global Medical Robotics market is expected to grow to $2.05 billion in 2014. Asia had the largest 32.3 % portion of the overall medical robotics market in 2008 at $329.27 million. The North American market was worth $648 million in medical robots and computer assisted surgery equipment (Godfrey, 2010).

Current Science (2010) states that in Jena, Germany, Martin Gross noticed his brother-in-law's three-legged dog had adapted to having three legs. Mr. Gross hopes to program Robots to function well even if a limb is lost. Mr. Gross is a researcher at the University of Jena in Germany. He belongs to the Locomorph

Association in Europe, which studies robotic locomotion. Robots are useful to researchers in many fields. In the

aeronautics field, Spirit explored the planet and Mars took photos and gathered evidence. It discovered

minerals, which means that Mars could have had life on it in the past. However, it is extremely hot because it is

close to the sun (Current Science, 2010).

The Robotic Operating Room

Stanton (2010) is proud to announce that health care facilities across the country continue to incorporate

robots into operating rooms. Hospitals are trying to update to robotic surgery to ensure faster recovery, less

pain, and less risk of infection. The key to creating a successful robotics program involves a patient safety,

staffing, and education. As of March 2010, St. Joseph's Hospital has done more than 1,500 robotic surgeries

utilizing four active robotic systems. One system is used for training. Perioperative registered nurses are chosen

to take on the role of robotic surgery coordinator. Each robotic patient has two IVs started to help prevent

difficulty gaining access during surgery, once the robot is placed. The Ohio Center for Advanced Robotic

Surgery program has done more than 4,200 procedures (Stanton, 2010).

Motoman Industrial Robots

Connolly (2009) reports that this study is to analyze Motoman's dual arm humanoid robot. In 2006,

Motoman is about the same size as a person. The robot is designed to assemble, handle, package, machine

tending, and parts transfer. Motoman is the robotic division of Yaskawa Electric Corporation, which was

founded in 1989. Motoman was launched in Japan in late 2005. Electrical wiring is located in the arms, and the

robot draws an average power of 4.2 kVA. The slim individual arm is a narrow arm robot with 20 kg payload

and seven axes. All operations such as programming and maintenance can be done through a pendant, and the

100-user password restricts access of the user. Advanced robotic motion control algorithms calculate axis torque and load in order to improve motion and speed. The INFORM programming language controls Motoman Robots (Connolly, 2009).

Connolly (2009) states that Motoman has introduced EasyLoad (TM) machine tending software of 2008 for the general public. EasyLoad then generates the program automatically through templates. The web site: www.lovingthemachine.com/2007/07/motoman-superannuates-you.html provides a demonstration. Motoman can sort and handle 1,000 packages an hour, which is faster than what most human workers can do. One of the videos on YouTube, at: www.youtube.com/watch?v=PSuvFCPgwE8, shows a Motoman Robotics (UK) Ltd stated that a robot can assemble a delicate camera in 4 to 5 hours. Two-arm robots are more costly than conventional robots, but they allow new possibilities. Motoman robots can hold with one hand and process with the other. Some interesting websites to view the Motoman Robot are the following:

1.) MOTOMAN Robotics UK Ltd, Banbury, UK - www.motoman.eu/uk

2.) Yaskawa Electric Corporation, Japan - www.yaskawa.co.jp/en

3.) YouTube videos of Motoman two-arm robots in action -

www.youtube.com/watch?v=PSuvFCPgwE8

4.) Industrial Robotics Research Group, Mechanical Engineering Department, University

of Coimbra, Portugal - http://robota.dem.uc.pt

5.) Hokusho Co. Ltd, Kanazawa-city, Ishikawa, Japan –

www.hokusho.co.jp/english/index.htm

6.) Automation IG, Chattanooga, TN, USA - www.automationig.com

(Connolly, 2009).

Robot Athletes

Cohen (2011) declares that imagination should be used to envision robots that can play soccer (football) at the level of the World Cup championships. In 1997, IBM's Deep Blue supercomputer defeated the world champion, Garry Kasparov in chess. Launched in 1993, the RoboCup international robot soccer competition (also known as the Robot World Cup Initiative) enables AI and robotics researchers to test their robots. French company Aldebaran created the Robot, Nao. This is the robot currently in use at the RoboCup. Nao robots use color cameras as their sensors, operate autonomously, and can communicate with each other wirelessly. Soccer is good for testing the basics that will be mandatory for urban search and rescue, and many other projects. Cohen encourages people to visit the website, RoboCup, www.robocup.org. (Cohen, 2011).

Terabyters

Frey (2011) declares that the trademark Gargoyle gear ™ is used by some people to sell information to the Internet. Some people sell information to server farms for search engines designed to show the physical world. The people wear object-recognition software, geospatial coordinates, and other sensory response data, which translates the physical world around a person into digital information that is searchable. These people are like spidering bots that tech companies currently use to scan the digital world to use some of the recorded information for advertisements (Frey, 2011).

Robots and Global Positioning System (GPS) Navigation

Berrabah, Baudoin, and Sahli (2010) declare that mobile robot positioning accuracy using a Simultaneous Localization and Mapping (SLAM) uses data from a single monocular camera together with data from Global Positioning System (GPS), Inertial Navigation System (INS) and wheel encoders for robot location in large-scale environments. Robot navigation in large outdoor environments is achieved by building several size limited local maps and combining them into a global map using a 'history' memory. This accumulates sensory evidence over time to identify places. The camera is attached to the robot. Data from GPS localizes the robot in satellite images. This research has been conducted successfully by the European research project View-Finder FP6 1ST 045541 (Berrabah, Baudoin, & Sahli, 2010).

Robots and Education

Chih-Wei, Jih-Hsien, Po-Yao, Chin-Yeh, and Gwo-Dong, (2010) state that robots can assist in teaching language by being interactive for teachers and students. Teachers can adjust the difficulty level. The robot can do the following: (1) gestures (2) change intonation or speed of speaking and (3) attract attention. The robot in this analysis was the robot toy, Robosapien, which costs 250 USD. According to Moore's law, technology will be less expensive over time. Teacher preparation maximizes learning ability. Students are more motivated to learn when the learning robot is interactive with them. Robots can also teach mathematics, and other subjects (Chih-Wei et Al., 2010).

Gordon (2011) declares that according to the federation, the population of service robots reached 63,000 units valued at $11 billion in 2008. Military, security, and rescue robots were 20,000 units in 2008. Robots are used for military drones, land robots that search for bombs; and surveillance robots. That is because robots cannot judge how far away objects are located. They lack the depth perception that most of us take for granted when we maneuver through everyday life. However, computer scientists at Stanford University recently came up -with a way to help the robots. All it takes is just one video camera, said Andrew Ng, an assistant professor of computer science at Stanford. To give robots depth perception, Ng and graduate students Ashutosh Saxena and Sung Chung designed software that is programmed into robots to see depth perception such as converging lines and haziness to mean distance (Gordon, 2011).

The International Robotics Exhibit

Kasuda (2008) declares that the purpose of this study is to review the iREX2007, the International Robot Exhibition 2007 held in Tokyo, Japan, with emphasis on new trends in the Japanese robotic industry. Robot creators need to listen to users. Robot users know that robots are a valuable tool. The 2007 International Robot Exhibition (www.irex2007.jp) was held in Tokyo. The exhibition lasted from November 28 to December 1, 2007. There were 199 companies and 66 organizations in the exhibition. The world's top manufacturing robot companies showed various robots. There were industrial robots for manufacturing and service robots for health care, security, and disaster recovery. The exhibition was a success. Interest was generated toward robotics. There were prototypes and toy-robots. There were plenty of biped walking robots for recreation and education. Microsoft showed the first Microsoft Robotics Studio in December 2006. It is a development kit that works on the windows operating system. Microsoft showed up in iREX2007 with Microsoft Robotics Studio. At Microsoft booth ZMP Inc., showed a biped robot developed on Microsoft Robotics Studio. Robots developed on Microsoft Robotics Studio can be controlled via a mobile phone (Kasuda, 2008).

Robots and NASA

Goetz et Al. (2010) state that the National Aeronautics and Space Administration (NASA) will provide video coverage featuring Curiosity team members. As of late October, workers added new to Curiosity rover. It has six wheels, and 7'-long robotic arms. Curiosity has been designed to drive longer distances over rougher land. Curiousity has a payload 10 times than previous rovers. The rover will ship to NASA's Kennedy Space Center in Florida next spring. The launch may happen between November 25 and December 18, 2011. It is planned to have Curiosity be on Mars in August 2012. Continuous live video is available at www. ustream.tv/channel/nasajpl (Goetz et Al., 2010).

Conclusion for Robots

Robots are beneficial to society. They are helpful and useful in performing tasks for human beings. In the medical field, robots are saving lives by performing minimally invasive surgery. Robots are doing surgical techniques that human beings are unable to perform alone. By using miniature cameras, robots can show a view inside a person's body. Other apparatus enables doctors to do certain actions with machines inside the patient's body. The wonderful concept is that the patient can heal in less time with less pain because it is minimally invasive. Robots can do just about anything; if they are programmed to do certain tasks. There are industrial robots that can assemble products such as cameras. Of course, robots have to be designed to be able to carry a certain amount of weight for different actions involved. Robots come in all sizes and shapes much like people do. The new robots can be just as agile as an athlete can, while playing soccer in Robocup for robots. Researchers can study robots while they are playing soccer. In a comparison of all the different researchers' robots, the Motoman Robot is by far the best robot currently. It is the best research in robotics because of the lightweight design that has many joints like a human being. This enables the robot to move agilely. Robots can even be programmed to think for themselves, and be autonomous (self-governing). However, robots must be programmed to do only good actions. A robot in the wrong researcher's hands can lead to much havoc. Robots can do many good actions in the world if programmed properly. Therefore, robots are beneficial to society.

Bionics and Artificial Computer Related Body Replacement Parts

Nature (2006) describes computer systems that enable a brain to control body parts are becoming reality. The following quote is from the 1970's television program called 'The Six Million Dollar Man': "Gentlemen, we can rebuild him. We have the technology," announced the narrator at the beginning. 'The Six Million Dollar Man' program showed scientists rebuilding the shattered body of a crash victim, Steve Austin, with bionic implants he could control with his brain. In the 1970's, this was just fantasy. However, two papers in this week's *Nature*

implicitly state that the direct communication of the human brain with computers or robots is no

longer within the parameters of science fiction. Both papers declare the development of electronic brain

implants, named neuroprostheses, which can translate the action to move a body part. The hope is to give

paralyzed patients movement, and to bypass damaged spinal cords. This is the result of many decades of

research from many industries such as computing, engineering and neurobiology (Nature, 2006).

Nature (2006) states that the Krishna Shenoy Group of Stanford University work with

monkeys that are not paralyzed. The Shenoy Group has found a technique to speed up the interface of brain and

machine. The progress that has happened is fantastic! However, some obstacles are in the way. The current

prosthesis is bulky and attached to a cart of equipment. A team of technicians needs to be present. The

prototype implant has wires that go into the skull and skin. Wireless signal transmission will be attempted to

avoid using wires. Steve Austin was re-created to have super strength, speed and vision. The idea of

superhuman powers appeals to many people. However, in reality, using neuroprosthetics will give paralyzed

patients movement and a normal life as much as possible (Nature, 2006).

Conception and Beneficial Computer Devices

Shamonki, Spandorfer, and Rosenwaks (2005) state that ultrasound is beneficial for the

placement of intrauterine fertilization transfer (IVF). The ultrasound hand device is placed on the stomach, and

can transmit a view of what is inside. Then, it is shown on the computer screen monitor for the doctor to see,

and implant the fertilized eggs inside the woman's uterus. The use of ultrasound has been shown to decrease

the incidence of difficult transfers (Sallam et al, 2002; Matorras et al, 2002). The placement of embryos in a

successful way is extremely high due to being able to view inside the uterus. In this study, the test results are as

follows: 19.4% of patients had a discrepancy of greater than or equal to 1.5 cm. and 29.9% had a discrepancy

of greater than or equal to one cm. during ultrasound guided transfer into the uterus. This allows for more accurate embryo placement. Therefore, this is much better than going in there without being able to view inside the uterine cavity (Shamonki, Spandorfer, & Rosenwaks, 2005).

Life Support Systems and Computer Devices

John et Al. (2009) declare that critical Care Services in modern medicine play a vital role in delivering prompt, appropriate and adequate care to acutely ill patients.

Survey Percentages are as follows:

1.) In 68 controlled studies of decision support systems between 1974 and 1992, computer-based

clinical decision support systems improved physician performance in 66%.

2.) In 70 studies, decision support systems again significantly improved clinical practice in 68% of trials.

3.) In 64% of the studies with higher (P = 0.02) success rates with automatic systems.

Intensive care units maintain a large amount of data in several areas such as cardiovascular, respiratory, neurological, and many more. This project was developed by intensivists and computer software teachers.

The name of the computer system is an acronym - CARDAMOM (Computer-Assisted recording, Diagnosis and Management of the Medically ill). This project was executed at the Christian

Medical College Hospital, Vellore, South India, the Computer Science Department, and the

Vellore Institute of Technology over a six-month period (June-November 2008).

The project was designed and developed in four phases such as the following:

Phase one - Monitoring and medication sheets; definitions

Phase two - Diagnostics and intervention bundle

Phase three - Testing of software

Phase four - Interfacing of investigations and monitoring data (John et Al., 2009).

John et Al. (2009) state that computer systems are being increasingly recognized as an important tool in the medical field. These computer information systems support a wide variety of tasks ranging from simple reminders to complex decisions. Such systems are extremely important in critical care. The difficulty of critical care and the many tasks that need to be performed for each patient leave room for errors and mistakes. Computer support systems that contain checklists, alerts, and diagnostics are currently utilized. Therefore, computerized life support systems improve the quality of care for everyone (John et Al., 2009).

Cryonics and Computer Devices to Restore Life Potentially to Deceased People

Harris and Wowk (2004) declare that cryonics is totally plausible and possible. In 1985, a paper showed successful vitrification of living cells (embryos). The embryos were cooled at a rate of 20° per minute. Chemicals are needed to replace water because freezing can damage cells in the body when the water turns to ice. A vitrified whole kidney in 1984 was successfully well frozen. There has been steady progress in reducing the toxicity of vitrification solutions since the modern concept of vitrification was first suggested by co-worker, Dr. Gregory Fahy, 20 years ago. Whole mammalian kidneys were cooled to -45° C using vitrification solutions and successfully transplanted. This work is described in the April 2004, issue of the journal Cryobiology, Brian Wowk, Ph.D., Sr. Scientist, 21^s Century Medicine, Inc., wowk@comcast.net. Dr. Wowk declares that slow cooling and warming rates are now possible because of newer antifreeze agents (Fahy, Wowk, Wu, Phan, Rasch, Chang, & Zendejas, 2004). "Cryopreservation of Organs by Vitrification: Perspectives and Recent Advances." Cryobiology 48: 157-178.   Toxicity issues will be overcome recovering a person from deep freeze cryonics and will entail a cure for severe antifreeze poisoning (Harris & Wowk, 2009).

Alcor (2010) states that Alcor is the best place to be frozen using the cryonics procedure. Cryonics is the process of using extremely cold temperatures to freeze people. The hope is that one day a cure will be found for whatever made the person die. The Alcor Life Extension Foundation has been open since 1972. Alcor is a non-profit organization. The organization is located in Scottsdale, Arizona (Alcor, 2010).

Alcor (2010) states that a heart lung machine is used to pump a sort of anti-freeze liquid into the person's circulatory system. The anti-freeze is called cryoprotectant solution. A computer system collects temperature, pressure, and concentration of cryoprotectant liquid data. The cryonics procedure takes four hours. After the liquid is pumped into the body, the person is then moved to the cooling room for vitrification. Vitrification is cooling a body down to -130 degrees Fahrenheit. Computers monitor the cooling process. After the vitrification cooling process, the body is placed in rust proof aluminum sealed containers. This container containing the cooled down body is then placed in another rocket-looking container that contains liquid nitrogen at -196 degrees Fahrenheit (Alcor, 2010).

Computer Devices Used in the Aerospace Industry

Eckhardt and Laith (2002) state that the use of computer simulation enables the building process to become more precise. Lockheed Martin engineers are utilizing CFD software to be sure of the correct climate inside the space vehicle. The engineers built a computer model of the X-38 and used CFD to simulate the airflow through the space vehicle's cabin. This eliminated the need and extra costs of building a prototype. The computer blocked airflow problems. The space vehicle is the X-38, which is designed on the International Space Station as an emergency vehicle such as a lifeboat of a ship. The X-38 program is to build a human spacecraft for a cost of approximately 90 million dollars. While in orbit, the surface temperature can change from 120 deg C to - 62 deg C. In the cold environment, condensation is a concern, as scientists learned from the experiences of the MIR space station. Moisture build up can cause damage to parts and fungus to grow

(Eckhardt & Laith, 2002).

Mandatory Laws to Promote the Use of Computer Devices that Provide Safety

Houston and Richardson (2009) state that safety on America's highways has been an extremely important issue. Congress has in the past pushed states to adopt lower speed limits, mandatory motorcycle helmet laws, and laws designed to deter driving under intoxication (DUI).

In 2006, a total of 41,642 fatal accidents happened on the America's highways, interstates, roads and streets. The totals are as follows:

A.) 32,092 were motor vehicle occupants

B.) 4,810 were motorcyclists

C.) 5,740 were non-occupants (such as pedestrians and cyclists) (Houston & Richardson, 2009). D.) Alcohol was a major factor in 17,602 of these fatalities.

E.) 86 percent involved an individual with a blood alcohol concentration (BAC) of 0.08 or higher.

F.) 1,794 children under the age of fourteen years died in 2006.

G.) 2.5 million nonfatal injuries

H.) $230.6 billion in economic costs for the United States for one year alone (National Highway Traffic Safety Administration (NHTSA) 2007) (Houston & Richardson, 2009).

Houston and Richardson (2009) declare that states have regulated speed limits, seat belt and child safety seat laws, motorcycle helmet laws, and drunk driving laws. States have some freedom to have certain laws. Congress has tried to motivate states to make laws (Cho and Wright 2004). The main motivation for achieving public health goals have been the use of fiscal tools. Congress commonly threatens states with the loss of federal highway construction funds if states do not adopt traffic safety laws [e.g., 55-mph speed limit, 21-year old minimum legal drinking age (MLDA), and the 0.08 BAC law (Houston & Richardson, 2009).

Houston and Richardson (2009) state that the speed limit law was enacted consequently because of the OPEC oil embargo related to the Middle East War of October 1973. Congress passed the Emergency Highway Energy Conservation Act (P.L. 93-239) which gave states sixty days to lower the maximum speed limits to 55 mph or risk the complete loss of federal highway funds. The sanctions were to remain in effect until June 1975. By the time, the sanctions were to take effect on March 4, 1974, all states had complied. In addition to fuel savings, a total of 9,100 fewer traffic fatalities happened in 1974 compared to 1973. This result led to the 55-mph maximum speed limit in the Federal-Aid Highway Amendments of 1974 (P.L. 93-643). Under this legislation, the law required only that the governor of each state certify that the state was making a serious effort to enforce highway speeds. Thirteen states had raised their maximum rural interstate speed limit to 70 mph, and eleven adopted 75 mph. In 1996, thirty-two states raised speed limits on roads other than rural interstates. Then, eleven raised speed limits. By August 2008, the 55 mph speed limit on rural interstate highways was just a memory (Houston & Richardson, 2009).

Houston and Richardson (2009) describe the 2005 Safe, Accountable, Flexible, and Efficient Transportation Equity Act. Legacy for Users (SAFETEA-LU, P.L. 109-59) gave $25 million over four years for child safety policies covering children up to eight years old. In comparison, the federal government has used a wider variety of tools and much greater funding as incentives to promote seat belts. Federal Motor Vehicle Safety Standard 208 (covering occupant crash protection) made it mandatory for vehicle manufacturers to install seatbelt systems or airbags by 1990. In 1995, all states except New Hampshire had a seat belt law (Houston & Richardson, 2009).

By: Tina Schaneville

Houston and Richardson (2009) describe the TEA-21 Act of 1998, Section 157 funds ($510 million over five years) distributed to states with seat belt use. Under section 406, $ 68 million of funds were to be distributed to states meeting conditions such as seat belt laws, and a child safety seat law. Studies show a 5.6 percentage point decrease (136 fewer fatalities) in the fatality rate for using seat belts (Houston & Richardson, 2009).

Houston and Richardson (2009) declare that at the end of 2005, forty-six states had helmet laws, of which twenty were universal coverage statutes. By 1987, forty-nine states had a minimum legal drinking age (MLDA) of twenty-one, and Wyoming complied in 1988. Congress has encouraged the 0.08 blood alcohol count (BAC) laws. Stiffer punishments are for BAC in the range above 0.15 (Houston & Richardson, 2009).

Houston and Richardson (2009) happily state that a tougher tool was used to force states to adopt the 0.08 BAC law in Section 163. Congress made it mandatory that a state adopt a 0.08 BAC law by October 2003 or lose 2 percent of federal highway funds in the first year. The second year 4 percent could have been lost. The third year could have been 6 percent. Finally, up to 8 percent annually could have been lost in FY2007. In addition, section 163 gave incentive grants ranging from $55 million in 1998 up to $90 million in 2001. By 2005, all states were in compliance. Not only does the federal government help for safety laws, but also the Mothers against Drunk Driving Organization are beneficial for stricter safety driving laws (Houston & Richardson, 2009).

Houston and Richardson (2009) emphatically declare that the federal government uses strong sanctions to encourage states to adopt driving under intoxication (DUI) driving laws, the minimum legal drinking age (MLDA) laws, and 0.08 blood alcohol count (BAC) laws. Hopefully, the state governments will be more inclined to adopt safety laws without having to have long struggles. That is one downfall of freedom. Sometimes, people want to be wild and have no regard for safety issues. Therefore, it makes absolute sense to obey laws, drive safely, and live life to the fullest without being incapacitated, disabled or deceased for the rest of your life. How will your family and friends get along without you? Make a difference in this world! Stand up for what is right and good (Houston & Richardson, 2009).

Ethics of New Technology

Anonymous (2009) asks two extremely important questions: Will robots be autonomous? Will they be lethal? (Anonymous, 2009). Currently, the robot functions as an associate that examines the battlefield. In the future, robots will be able to detect enemy fire and return it. Engineers must program robots with the laws of war to prevent unwanted deaths, and to do what is right for the United States of America. Terrorists may be less motivated to strike an enemy's territory if they have fewer chances of harming human soldiers. Computers and technology can give a person the power to see his victim, but experience none of the injuries or even avoid death (Anonymous, 2009).

The Lighter Side of Computers for Enjoyment & Computer Devices in Appliances

To Make Life Easier in Many Ways

Cell Phones and the Mobile Internet

Kroski (2008) conveys that most of us are using our cell phones primarily for emergency calls, and to chat with friends and relatives. However, people can access the Internet to receive: weather information, travel schedules, news reports, text in a pizza order to Domino's, borrow e-books from an online library; tour of a museum; watch Http://www.abcnews.com; and upload photos. People can do these actions with the Internet. The mobile Internet is extremely useful to anyone (Kroski, 2008).

Kroski (2008) is elated to state that the mobile Internet is the World Wide Web accessed through a cell phone, or other mobile device. Fifty percent of the world's population or 3.3 billion people are using a mobile Internet. The Pew Internet & American Life Project shows 32% of Americans access the mobile Web on a daily basis, and 58% have tried these applications at least once. Forrester Research provides a study that states that over half of Latinos and 50% of African Americans use their cell phones for data transfer (Kroski, 2008).

Kroski, (2008) acknowledges the benefits of the Mobile Web, which are the following:

* Constant Connectivity to Internet.

* Global positioning system (GPS)

* Limitless Access to the whole Internet (Kroski, 2008).

Types of Cell Phones

1.) Boost Mobile Cell Phone Service and the Incognito Cell Phone

Not all phone service companies offer as much as Boost Mobile 'Monthly Unlimited'. The cell phone service corporation is nationwide in 15,800 U.S. cities. Boost mobile has no extra fees such as roaming and long distance. The Boost Mobile network works hard to make sure there are no dropped calls. Boost Mobile's monthly-unlimited plan requires no contract. The corporation does not have to worry about losing customers because the corporation offers excellent service at the lowest prices possible. Boost Mobile allows payment flexibility with different plans. Boost Mobile operates on the Nextel National Network. Boost Mobile customers are able to call nationwide.

To sign up for Boost Monthly Unlimited: 1.) need a compatible Boost Mobile phone 2.) activate the account. To sign up, visit boostmobile.com or call 1-888-BOOST- 4U. In order to add money to the account, customers can pay with cash, re-boost card, or credit/debit cards. Customers can pay in person, online, or over

the phone. In order to keep the account active, the total monthly payment amount must be prepaid each month.

McKeen and Price (2010) declare that there is plenty competition in smartphones. The list of features can

confuse almost anyone. Different operating systems, applications, and many other features to decipher exist.

Then, the ABA Journal asked two intelligent people, Finis R. Price III and Ryan C. McKeen, to examine

features of the hottest brands: Apple's iPhone and Google's Android operating system. These two people just

happen to be attorneys stating the case for the brand that was chosen by each person (McKeen & Price, 2010).

McKeen and Price (2010) state that the Iphone and the Droid work very similar. The two types of

phones act very similar. However, the Iphone has 70,000 more applications than Google's Droid smartphone.

Furthermore, the Iphone can simultaneously access the Internet and put a client on speakerphone, which the

Droid cannot do. The Droid wins for battery life. The Droid has 6.4 hours of talk time and the Iphone has 5

hours. The Droid has a better camera than the Iphone and the Blackberry phone. The camera comparison is as

follows: Droid has a 5-megapixel camera; the Iphone a 3-megapixel camera; and the Blackberry has a 2-

megapixel camera. The Droid and Blackberry have a flash built in, and the Iphone does not. The Droid has a

larger and clearer screen. The Droid is easier for typing with an actual keyboard. The Iphone does not have a

keyboard. The Iphone's keyboard comes up and is part of the flat screen. The Iphone can access Itunes, and the

Droid can access amazon's song collection online. Both have sufficient security measures built into the cell

phones. Both the iPhone and the Droid cost $199 with a two-year service contract, or $599 without. Therefore,

the Droid is the best cell phone because it has a larger screen, a better battery, a physical keyboard, a better

camera, and uses a compatible Microsoft operating system (McKeen & Price, 2010).

Appliances

Igaki, Matsumoto, Nakamura, Tamada, & Tanaka (2008) state that innovative technologies enable

general household appliances, such as TVs, DVD players, lights, ventilators, refrigerators, air conditioners, blinds and curtains, to be connected to a computer at home. This type of system is generally called a home network system (HNS), which is capable of providing more convenient and comfortable living for home users. Research and development of home network systems are already on the market, (e.g., Hitachi, 2003; Matsushita, 2005; Toshiba, 2005). Home network systems provide many applications and services such as wide-range control and monitoring of appliances inside and outside the home. Appliances are equipped with a network interface, a processor and storage, in order to provide and execute the appliance features (Igaki et Al., 2008).

Igaki, Matsumoto, Nakamura, Tamada, & Tanaka (2008) declare that a home network system consists of one or more networked appliances connected to a local area network (LAN). Communications among the appliances are executed based on network protocol. Currently, many protocols are being standardized for the networked appliances. Major protocols include DLNA (DLNA, 2006) for digital audio/video appliances and ECHONET (ECHONET, 2006) for refrigerators, air conditioners, and laundry machines. Many programming languages such as Perl and Java can be used quite effectively. Different platforms can be used such as Windows, Linux, and Sun Solaris (Igaki et Al., 2008).

The Dell Laptop

Dell Corporation (2010) states that the Dell personal computer was introduced in 1986, and has influenced the industry. Dell's research and development (R&D) can be found worldwide. Some of the best intelligent people are contributing to the design and engineering of a Dell product. Dell takes into account the customer's needs; which is the basis for Dell Corporation's success. The Dell Corporation gathers customers' ideas from the following: interactions, organized events, and customer surveys. Partnerships from software, hardware and other suppliers give information that is even more valuable. Many innovations start in-house. Dell Corporation employs a global team of top engineers, product designers and technical experts. Other people's ideas come from a team effort with Dell's strategic partners. The mission is to deliver innovative and cost-effective solutions that meet what the customer needs and wants (Dell, 2010).

Dell Corporation (2010) declares that the Dell Corporation impacts society because it is usually one of the first companies to provide new features on computers. By sharing ideas globally, the Dell Corporation is always one of the first corporations to provide new features. Sharing ideas is more important than competing. New knowledge from anywhere is always viewed and taken into consideration. Therefore, the Dell Corporation promotes innovation to deliver new and improved products to consumers. The Dell Corporation (2010) states that people worldwide can purchase Dell online, by phone, and more than 50,000 outlets (Dell, 2010).

Dell Corporation (2010) showcased new products on January 7th, 2010 at the CES Show in Las Vegas, Nevada, the Dell Corporation exhibited the following products:

- Mini 3 smart phone and 5-inch tablet concept
- Dell's first ultra-mobile gaming laptop - the Alienware M11x (Dell, 2010).

Dell Corporation (2010) realizes that the Dell Corporation is entering the age of mobilization. People desire to have mobile products that help them stay connected; utilize the latest tools, and services for effective digital experiences while traveling. The Dell Corporation is focused on technology that benefits people to connect virtually anytime and anywhere. Consumers are demanding mobility in high-quality devices. The Dell Corporation will utilize U.S. AT&T cellular company for the Mini 3 Android based smart phone (Dell, 2010).

Dell Corporation (2010) states the Dell Corporation's results from a study of more than 1,500 people about smart phones stated that 82 percent would not leave home without the smart phone. More than half of those surveyed said they wanted to choose from a wider variety of smart phones. For more information on the survey visit Dell Official Flicker page (Dell, 2010).

Dell Corporation (2010) provides a glimpse of Dell's new products, which include the following:

- The Alienware M11x, the most powerful 11-inch gaming laptop in the universe

- A refreshed Studio 14 laptop for individuals who create and consume digital content

New versions of the Inspiron PC line, Intel's new Core i5 processors, and "smart" features in Turbo Boost technology are available. Visit Http://www.dell.com for the newest products (Dell, 2010).

Dell Corporation (2010) declares more new products:

Alienware M11x

- The Alienware M11x demonstrates high graphics power

Alienware OptX™ AW2310 23" 3D Full HD Widescreen Monitor

- The 23" Alienware OptX™ AW2310 provides an immersive stereoscopic 3D experience

- Enable intense stereoscopic 3D effects on hundreds of PC game titles with NVIDIA® 3D Vision™ technology

- Price for monitor is $499 (NVIDIA 3D Vision Kit not included)

- The most powerful 17-inch and 15-inch Alienware gaming laptops ever created

- The M17x, the most powerful 17-inch gaming laptop in the universe, provides Intel Core i7 processors combined with dual graphics to give extreme frame rates at high-density resolutions at high game settings.

- The M15x gives exceptional HD video and audio editing, 3D animation and high-end PC gaming

M17x start at $1,799 and the M15x start at $1,399.

Inspiron 14, 15, 17

- Redesigned Inspiron laptops for mobile media

- thinner chassis, 16:9 aspect HD displays, SRS Premium Sound™

- turbo-charged Intel® Core™ i5 processors starting at $849.

- Systems featuring the Intel Core i3 processor, starting at $569.

Inspiron 580, 580s

- great, high-value desktop computers

- desktop line with new processors, and color choices. Prices start at $269.

Studio 14, 15, 17

- Refreshed Studio laptops feature Intel Core i5 and i7 processors for sharing photos, music and videos with friends and family.

- Portable Studio 14, starting at $699.

- Studio 15 has high-definition, 15.6-inch LED widescreen design and is rich with multimedia technology, like True HD resolutions, starting at $849

- Studio 17 features beautiful 17.3-inch display, with audio. Prices start at $949.

Studio XPS 8100

- a high-performance, multi-purpose desktop computer

- Replaces Studio XPS 8000 with Intel Core i5 processor technology, new theater-quality THX® TruStudio PC™ sound and design. Prices start at $749.

*Stereoscopic 3D requires optional NVIDIA® 3D Vision™ Kit and a desktop system with Dual-Link DVI

Ports and a compatible NVIDIA graphics solution. For a full list of system requirements, please visit:

http://www.nvidia.com/object/GeForce_3D_Vision_Requirements.html. To view the newest computer products visit Http://www.dell.com (Dell, 2010).

Innovation

Venkat (2010) declares that companies take ideas for Research & Development from the general public. Many people contribute ideas such as customers, managers, front-line employees, partners and all other stakeholders. The French telecom firm, Orange, and the California-based global networking firm, Cisco, have gained competitive advantage from using the co-creative enterprise business concept to generate profits. The focus of the approach at Orange is on environments with customers and industry workers, and at Cisco it is on risk and reward (Venkat, 2010).

Venkat (2010) states that the Orange Corporation has opened up its Research &Development process to the outside world through its web-based program, which provides many different kinds of information. The Lab enables the submission of Business-to-Business (B2B) ideas and product proposals. Such access to information is necessary for potential external partners working on prototypes. Orange has received many ideas through Livebox Lab and has already initiated several products through this channel. One idea from the public is LiveRadio, a Wi-Fi device enabling the streaming of hundreds of Web-radio channels (Venkat, 2010).

Venkat (2010) shows that the Cisco Corporation provides a view into the creative program. It investigates how a large global corporation displays innovation. It is a collaborative and organizational change. Sustaining innovation mandates that leaders in any organization guide the structuring of creative abilities inside the corporations. Leaders must engage numerous stakeholders in the network to bring about large-scale innovation. They must also learn to manage the process of innovation with stakeholders inside and outside the corporation (Venkat, 2010).

Venkat (2010) summarizes the basic benefits of the new Cisco structure for its customers. Corporations must now take a path from one of the boards when introducing or withdrawing a prototype product. Moreover, performance management has now become a collectively shared process. Many people inside the board of the corporation are accountable for managing products and performance. Therefore, many people collaborate on an idea to test the feasibility of mass production before wasting many monetary funds (Venkat, 2010).

Sato (2009) realizes that design research helps establish a benchmark for what customers deem worthy in life. Design thinking is a standard that balances customer, business and technology needs to ensure that results benefit everyone. Design teams guided in design thinking by experts will invent powerful innovations. To create excellent products from concepts, execution of mass production benefits the corporation and customers. Current designers are trained to use design thinking to strike this balance as this transforms concepts into profits. Therefore, designers play a key role in integrating the contributions of everyone into the best prototype possible. To make this a reality, there is a shared network to design roles for planning and execution. The framework ties the goal of design into business consequences (Sato, 2009).

Desouza, Dombrowski, Awazu, Baloh, Papagari, Jha, & Kim (2009) declare that 'innovation' is a subject that is well planned at many corporations. The need to innovate effectively and efficiently is mandatory to last and grow in a strong competitive marketplace. In today's competitive economy, corporations that have strategic processes for innovation will lead the industries. New corporations, such as Google and Amazon, have been successful at innovating at rates faster than many other corporations innovate. Traditional corporations are handling innovation well, also. These corporations change according to economic conditions and execute innovative strategies in effective ways (Desouza et Al., 2009).

Desouza et Al. (2009) state that General Electric (GE) is well known for successful ways of generating innovation. Lunar, a Wisconsin-based company collaborated with GE on portable bone density scanners.

Working with GE gave Lunar greater access to markets. GE Healthcare benefited by obtaining a percentage of profits from Lunar. The new technology can test for percentage of body fat (Newman, 2006) (Desouza, et Al., 2009).

Desouza et Al. (2009) state that Whirlpool had been known for its focus on building high-quality products while keeping costs down in innovation. In 2000, they created a new vision for customer-centered innovation: 'a creative idea focused on a customer touch point that: creates unique and compelling solutions valued by the customer; creates real and sustainable competitive advantage; creates extraordinary value for Whirlpool shareholders; comes from everywhere and anyone' (Cutler, 2003). These points emphasize a.) stakeholders - especially customers and b.) democratic innovation. Whirlpool focused on idea generation, advocacy for customer needs and marketing; organizational learning, mentors/ sponsors, and alliances with other retailers as well as suppliers. Information technologies were utilized throughout the innovative process. Mentors and sponsors supported and assisted the people who innovated. Prior to rolling out the focus on innovation, new executive-level positions (such as the VP of leadership and competency creation) were created (Melymuka, 2004). Top management supported the innovation process every step of the way, from providing funding (20-35% of the annual budget was intended to be spent on innovation and innovation processes in 2001- 2003) to featuring slogans such as, 'Thinking outside the box, inside the home' in the annual report (Richard, 2002). Whirlpool's culture can be described as an 'innovation democracy' (Melymuka, 2004) because anyone may participate. Top management's unwavering support for the technology infrastructure, slogans promoting the innovative process, and seed funding for pilot projects contributed to the development of a highly collaborative and innovative culture, which enabled Whirlpool to outperform competitors (Desouza et Al., 2009).

THE INNOVATION PROCESS

Desouza et. Al. (2009) state the innovation process, which is the following: generation and mobilization, advocacy and screening, experimentation, commercialization, and diffusion and implementation. The stages are in a cycle. An idea has stages before it is executed by a corporation. The stages of the innovation process detail the steps that an idea must go through to become fully executed. The process is different at different corporations. However, the process is basically the same (Desouza et Al., 2009).

Conclusion: How New Technology Affects Society Wonderfully

In conclusion, there are industrial robots that can assemble products such as cameras. Of course, robots have to be designed to be able to carry a certain amount of weight for different actions involved. Robots come in all sizes and shapes much like people do. The new robots can be just as agile as an athlete can, while playing soccer in Robocup for robots. Researchers can study robots while they are playing soccer. In a comparison of all the different researchers' robots, the Motoman Robot is by far the best robot currently. It is the best research in robotics because of the lightweight design that has many joints like a human being. This enables the robot to move agilely. Robots can even be programmed to think for themselves, and be autonomous (self-governing). However, robots must be programmed to do only good actions. A robot in the wrong researcher's hands can lead to much havoc. Robots can do many good actions in the world if programmed properly. Therefore, high technology is beneficial to society.

Laws must be enacted to keep up with the dynamic and ever-changing pace of high technology. High technology can be utilized for good actions; only if laws that control high technology are created for the betterment of society as a whole. High technology must never be utilized for secretive, illegal actions. Any action that is secretive is considered evil. Honesty is always the best policy for all parties involved. If a party does not want to participate, then that should be respected. Respect and love of others is what Jesus Christ and

By: Tina Schaneville

the Creator of the Universe stated over 2000 years ago in a city called Bethlehem. Jesus stated, "Do unto others as you would do unto yourself" (Jesus Christ, 33 A.D.).

High technology is extremely beneficial to society. Many mechanical devices, robots, machinery and automobiles have computers inside to control for safety and other functions. For example, robots are beneficial and useful in performing tasks for human beings. In the medical field, robots are saving lives by performing minimally invasive surgery. Robots are doing surgical techniques that human beings are unable to perform alone. By using miniature cameras, robots can show a view inside a person's body. Other apparatus enables doctors to do certain actions with machines inside the patient's body. The wonderful concept is that the patient can heal in less time with less pain because it is minimally invasive. Robots can do just about anything; if they are programmed to do certain tasks. In Canada, computer assisted head surgery is performed on Canadian ambulances that ride to vehicle accidents to offer much needed, life-saving head surgery (Shen, Shen, & Gu 2007). A hole is drilled into the skull to let the blood out so no pressure is placed on the brain. Then, the patient is airlifted in a helicopter to the nearest hospital. The critical life-saving minutes of this extremely valuable head surgery saves many critically injured people who would have died had they not received this procedure on the scene of the accident. Time is critical and of the utmost importance in saving lives. NO ONE HAS TO DIE!

References

Albu-Schäffer, Haddadin, S, Ch. Ott; Stemmer, A., & T. Wimböck, et al. (2007). The DLR

Lightweight Robot: design and control concepts for robots in human environments. The Industrial

Robot, 34(5), 376-385. Retrieved on February 9, 2011 from

http://search.proquest.com.ezproxy.apollolibrary.com/docview/217016034/fulltext/12D76BB7C2E73260224/48

?accountid=35812.

Alcor Organization. (2010). The Alcor Organization. Retrieved from Http://www.alcor.org. on April 19, 2010.

Anonymous. Wired for War: The Robotics Revolution and Conflict in the 21st Century. (2009). Ethics &

International Affairs, 23(3), 312-313. Retrieved April 20, 2010, from Research Library.

(Document ID: 1878361991).

Baker, A. (1987). In Car Alcohol Breath Analyzer-A Pilot Study, Safety Education Centre, College Park,

Maryland. Beck, K.H., Rauch, W.J. and Baker, E.A. (1997). The Effects of Alcohol Ignition

Interlock License Restrictions on Multiple Offenders: A Randomized Trial in Maryland,

Insurance Institute for Highway Safety, Virginia.

Bales, William D., Blomberg, Thomas G., & Kathy G. Padgett. (2006). Under Surveillance: An Empirical Test

of the Effectiveness and Consequences of Electronic Monitoring. Criminology & Public

Policy, 5(1), 61- 91. Retrieved March 28, 2010, from Research Library. (Document

ID: 1016637751).

Beirness, D.J. and Simpson, H.M. (1991). Alcohol Ignition Interlocks: Their Function and Role in

Preventing Impaired Driving, The Traffic Injury Research Foundation of Canada, Ontario.

Beirness, D., Simpson, H.& Mayhew, D. (1998). Programs and policies for reducing

alcohol-related motor vehicle deaths and injuries, Contemporary Drug Problems, 25(3), 553-571.

Berrabah, S, Baudoin, Y., & Sahli, H. (2010). Multi-Sensor SLAM Approach

for Robot Navigation Sensors & Transducers, 9, 200-213. Retrieved on February 9, 2011

from http://search.proquest.com.ezproxy.apollolibrary.com/docview/840577800/fulltext/12D72C5D0DB565A19

3B/5

2? accountid=35812.

Billiot Jr., Charles J. (2012). Photos of Charie Ann Billiot, Chrissie Ann Billiot,

& Brian James Lafontaine. Retrieved from Chuck Billiot Photography,

located in Mandeville, Louisiana. Website: http://www.chuckbilliot.com.

Brown, A. (2010). Industrial Robots Fall: Service Robots Gain.Mechanical Engineering 132.1 (Jan 2010): 18.

Retrieved on February 9, 2011

from http://search.proquest.com.ezproxy.apollolibrary.com/docview/230174747/fulltext/12D76BB7C2E732602

24/51

?accountid=35812.

Brown, A. (2009). Robot Population Explosion. Mechanical Engineering, 131(2), 64. Retrieved April 12,

2010, from ABI/INFORM Global. (Document ID: 1638760581).

Boost Mobile. (2010). Boost Mobile Monthly Cell Phone Service. Retrieved on May 2, 2010 from

http://boostmobilecommunity.com/ReadMore.aspx?blogid=486&cid=HP_Promo_Tray_Monthly_Unlimited.

Busch, C. (2006). Facing the future of biometrics: Demand for safety and security in the

public and private sectors is driving research in this rapidly growing field. EMBO Reports, 7(SI).

Retrieved April 4, 2010, from Research Library. (Document ID: 1071194351).

Cargo GSA Network. (2010). Advanced Female Android Aiko Created By Le Trung in Canada in 2007.

Retrieved on April 12, 2010 from http://cargogsanetwork.com/advance-female-android-aiko-ai-robot-

fembot.

Cavaiola, A., & Wuth, C. Assessment and Treatment of the DUI Offender. New York: Haworth, 2002.

Chih-Wei, C., Jih-Hsien, L., Po-Yao, C., Chin-Yeh, W., & Gwo-Dong, C. (2010). Exploring the

Possibility of Using Humanoid Robots as Instructional Tools for Teaching a Second Language in

Primary School. Journal of Educational Technology & Society, 13(2), 13-24. Retrieved from

EBSCOhost.

Cieslak, D. & Van Winkle, M. (2004). Carry Your Office in the Palm of Your Hand. Journal of

Accountancy, 198(2), 52-56. Retrieved May 2, 2010, from ABI/INFORM Global. (Document

ID: 678637721.

Cohen, A. (2011). Robots as Athletes. The Futurist. 45(1), 9-10. Retrieved on February

9, 2011 from

http://search.proquest.com.ezproxy.apollolibrary.com/docview/811085831/fulltext/12D7

2C5D0DB565A193B/9?accountid=35812.

Collier, D., Comeau, F. & Marples, I. (1995). Experience in Alberta with highly sophisticated anti-

circumvention features in a fuel cell based ignition interlock, Proceedings of the 13th International

Conference on Alcohol, Drugs and Traffic Safety, Adelaide, Australia, pp.673-677.

Connolly, C. (2009). Motoman Markets Co-operative and Humanoid Industrial Robots.

The Industrial Robot, 36(5), 417-420. Retrieved on February 9, 2011 from

http://search.proquest.com.ezproxy.apollolibrary.com/docview/217005594/fulltext/12D7

2AA6DB06D5F4479/7? accountid=35812.

Coxon, G. & Earl, R. (1998). Riverland Alcohol Ignition Interlock Trial. Safety Strategy Report

Series 6/98, Transport South Australia, South Australia.

Current Science. (2010). Three-legged Dog Inspires Robotic Research. Current Science, 96 (5), 12-13. Retrieved

on February 9, 2011 from

http://search.proquest.com.ezproxy.apollolibrary.com/docview/848787497/12D76BB7C2

E73260224/11? accountid=35812.

Dell Corporation. Innovation. Retrieved on May 17th, 2010 from http://content.dell.com/us/en/corp/d/corp-comm/cto-customer-driven-innovation.aspx#.

Desouza, K., Dombrowski, C., Awazu, Y., Baloh, P., Papagari, S., Jha, S., & Kim, J.. (2009). Crafting organizational innovation processes. Innovation : Management, Policy & Practice, 11(1), 6-33. Retrieved July 12, 2010, from ABI/INFORM Global. (Document ID: 1701519641).

Dill, PH.D, P., & Wells-Parker PH.D, E.(2006). Alcohol Research and Health. Washington: (29), 41 - 8.

Eckhardt, B., & Laith, Z. (2002). Computer simulation helps keep down costs for NASA's "lifeboat" for the international space station. Aircraft Engineering and Aerospace Technology, 74(5), 442. Retrieved April 20, 2010, from ABI/INFORM Trade & Industry. (Document ID: 220159541).

Etzold, L. (2011). Using Robots in Ballast Tanks: Project Under Way to Automate Inspection of Surface Prep and Coating Work. Journal of Protective Coatings & Linings, 28 - 36. Retrieved on February 10, 2011 from http://search.proquest.com.ezproxy.apollolibrary.com/docview/848435520/fulltext/12D7 6BB7C2E73260224/2? accountid=35812.

Francis, Erica. "A wake-up call behind the wheel." Forbes Autos. November 26, 2007. http://www.forbesautos.com/news/features/2007/sleeping-at-the-wheel.html.

Frey, T. (2011). The Coming of the Terabyters: Life logging for a Living. The Futurist. 45(1), 35-36. Retrieved on February 9, 2011 from http://search.proquest.com.ezproxy.apollolibrary.com/docview/811093617/fulltext/12D7 2C5D0DB565A193B/12?accountid=35812.

Godfrey, A. (2010). Robotic Technology Speeds Recovery and Improves Outcomes. JAAPA: Journal of the American Academy of Physician Assistants, 23(10), 53-4. Retrieved on February 9, 2011 from http://search.proquest.com.ezproxy.apollolibrary.com/docview/808050069/fulltext/12D7

23771FB65172647/15?accountid=35812.

Goetz, W., Pike, W., Hviid, S., Madsen, M., & Morris, R., et Al. (2010). Microscopy

Analysis of Soils at the Phoenix Landing Site, Mars. Journal of Geophysical Research.

Planets 115. Retrieved on February 9, 2011 from

http://search.proquest.com.ezproxy.apollolibrary.com/docview/749995732/fulltextPDF/1

2D77A727073B7DB384/9?accountid=35812. Gordon, Anne. (2011). Careers Inspired by Nanotech

Trends.

Gordon, Larry Dale. (2010). Drowsy Driver Alert Systems. Retrieved from:

http://auto.howstuffworks.com/car-driving-safety/safety-regulatory-devices/car-wake-you-up1.html.

Harris, Steven B. and Wowk, Brian. (2004). Cryonics Forum. Skeptic, 11(2), 27. Retrieved April 18, 2010,

from Research Library. (Document ID: 760354681).

Houston, D., & Richardson, L. (2009). Federalism and Safety on America's Highways. Publius, 39(1), 117-137.

Retrieved April 20, 2010, from Research Library. (Document ID: 1625350441).

Igaki, H., Matsumoto, K., Nakamura, M., Tamada, H., & Tanaka, H. (2008). Constructing Home Network

Systems and Integrated Services Using Legacy Home Appliances and Web Services. International

Journal of Web Services Research, 5(1), 82-98. Retrieved April 25, 2010, from ABI/INFORM

Global. (Document ID: 1523800401).

Is this the bionic man? (2006). Nature, 442(7099), 109. Retrieved April 12, 2010, from Research

Library. (Document ID: 1076577351).

John, P., Chacko, P., Rao, S., George, A., Anouncia, S., & Siromoney. (2009). A computer-assisted recording,

diagnosis and management of the medically ill system for use in the intensive care unit: A

preliminary report. Indian Journal of Critical Care Medicine, 13(3), 136-142. Retrieved April 18,

2010, from ProQuest Health and Medical Complete. (Document ID: 1939512081).

Kazi, R., Garg, A., & Dwivedi, R. (2010). Perspective on Robotic Surgery and

its Role in Head and Neck Cancers. Journal of Cancer Research and Therapeutics, 6(3),

237-238. Retrieved on February 9, 2011 from

http://search.proquest.com.ezproxy.apollolibrary.com/docview/850852144/fulltext/12D7

7A727073B7DB384/13?accountid=35812.

Krassioukov, Andrei et Al. (2011). Using Robot-Applied Resistance to Augment Body-Weight-

Supported Treadmill Training in an Individual with Incomplete Spinal Cord Injury.

Physical Therapy. 91(1), 143-151. Retrieved on February 9, 2011 from

http://search.proquest.com.ezproxy.apollolibrary.com/docview/846755110/fulltext/12D7

15BF4292DB5D632/6? accountid=35812.

Kroski, E. (2008). What Is the Mobile Web? Library Technology Reports, 44(5), 5-9. Retrieved April 25, 2010,

from Research Library. (Document ID: 1547999521).

Kusuda, Y. (2008). Robots at the International Robot Exhibition 2007 in Tokyo.

The Industrial Robot, 35(4), 300-306. Retrieved on February 9, 2011 from

http://search.proquest.com.ezproxy.apollolibrary.com/docview/217007378/fulltext/12D7

6BB7C2E73260224/57? accountid=35812.

Lakhani, Nagy, & Shih. (2010). Is Android or iPhone the Platform for Innovation in Imaging

Informatics? Journal of Digital Imaging, 23(1), 2-7. Retrieved May 2, 2010, from ProQuest Health

and Medical Complete. (Document ID: 1945925591).

"Lane departure warning systems help drowsy drivers avoid crashes." Science Daily. October 17, 2006.

http://www.sciencedaily.com/releases/2006/10/061016121708.html.

Marques, Voas, & Tippetts. (2003). Behavioral measures of drinking: Patterns from the Alcohol

Interlock Record. Addiction 98(Suppl. 2):13-19, 2003. PMID: 14984238.

McKeen, R., & Price, F. (2010). DROID v iPHONE. ABA Journal, 96(4), 56-62. Retrieved May 2, 2010, from

ABI/INFORM Global. (Document ID: 2007090141).

Michelini, Rinaldo & Razzoli, Roberto . (2008). Co-operative Minimally Invasive Robotic Surgery.

   The Industrial Robot, 35(4), 347-360. Retrieved on February 9, 2011 from

   http://search.proquest.com.ezproxy.apollolibrary.com/docview/217005251/fulltext/12D7

   1A83F2F71D8302/35?accountid=35812.

Peckham, S. (2010). View Assembly of Mars Rover Online. Tech Directions, 70(5), 8.

   Retrieved on February 9, 2011 from

   http://search.proquest.com.ezproxy.apollolibrary.com/docview/819261134/fulltext/12D7

   7A727073B7DB384/2?accountid=35812.

Popkin, C., Stewart, J., Martell, C., & Birchmayer, J. (1992). An evaluation of the effectiveness of the

   interlock in preventing recidivism in a population of multiple DWI offenders, Highway Safety

   Research Centre: Chapel Hill.

Matorras, R., Urquijo, E. & Mendoza, R. (2002). Ultrasound Guided Embryo Transfer improves pregnancy

   rates, and increases the frequency of easy transfers. Human Reproduction 17, 1762 - 1766.

Salisbury, J. (1998). The Heart of Microsurgery. Mechanical Engineering, 120(12), 46-

   51. Retrieved on February 9, 2011 from

   http://search.proquest.com.ezproxy.apollolibrary.com/docview/230176044/fulltextwithgr

   aphics/12D71A83F2F71D8302/23?accountid=35812.

Sallam, H., Agamaya, A., & Rahman, A. (2002). Ultrasound Measurement of the Uterocervical

   Angle before embryo Transfer: A Prospective Controlled Study. Human Reproduction 17, 1767-

   1772.

Sanderson, K. (2010). Mars Rover Spirit (2003-10). Nature, 463(7281) 600. Retrieved on February

   9, 2011 from

http://search.proquest.com.ezproxy.apollolibrary.com/docview/204545643/fulltext/12D7

77AD0A42AF56C0A/30?accountid=35812.

Santoro, Matteo, Marino, Dante, & Tamburrini, Gueglielmo. (2008). Learning Robots

Interacting with Humans. A.I. Society. 22(3), 301- 314. Retrieved on February 9, 2011

from http://search.proquest.com.ezproxy.apollolibrary.com/docview/223773404/fulltextPDF/1

2D76BB7C2E73260224/114? accountid=35812.

Sato, S. (2009). Beyond good: great innovations through design. The Journal of Business Strategy, 30(2/3), 40-

49. Retrieved July 12, 2010, from ABI/INFORM Global. (Document ID: 1876210541).

Seven Types of Service Robots. (2010). Industrial Automation Market Research Report, (p.52-

24). Markets and Markets. Retrieved February 09, 2011, from General OneFile via Gale:

http://find.galegroup.com.ezproxy.apollolibrary.com/gps/start.do?prodId=IPS&userGroupName=uphoenix.

Shamonki, M., Spandorfer, S., & Rosenwaks, Z. (2005). Ultrasound-guided embryo transfer and

the accuracy of trial embryo transfer. Human Reproduction, 20(3), 709-16. Retrieved April 18,

2010,   from Research Library. (Document ID: 800021621).

Shen, Y., Shen, W., & Gu, J. (2007). Sliding-mode Control for Tele-robotic Neurosurgical System.

International Journal of Robotics & Automation, 22(1), 19-31. Retrieved on February 9,

2011 from

http://search.proquest.com.ezproxy.apollolibrary.com/docview/218856438/fulltext/12D7

1A83F2F71D8302/34?accountid=35812.

Stanton, C. (2010). Association of Operating Room Nurses. AORN Journal. 92(6), 113-

115. Retrieved on February 9, 2011 from
http://search.proquest.com.ezproxy.apollolibrary.com/docview/815969887/fulltextPDF/1

2D72C5D0DB565A193B/31?accountid=35812.

"Tech watch: Volvo's driver alert control finally ready for prime time." Edmunds. August 30, 2007, retrieved on

March 28, 2010 from http://www.edmunds.com/insideline/do/News/articleId=122411.

The Futurist, 45(1), 38-39. Retrieved on February 9, 2011 from

http://search.proquest.com.ezproxy.apollolibrary.com/docview/811094980/fulltext/12D7

2C5D0DB565A193B/13?accountid=35812.

Thilmany, J. (2006). What the Robots See. Mechanical Engineering, 128(4), 64. Retrieved on February 9,

2011 from

http://search.proquest.com.ezproxy.apollolibrary.com/docview/230177438/fulltextwithgr

aphics/12D76BB7C2E73260224/45?accountid=35812.

Thompson, L. (2008). Security and the Internet: Fighting malware. Organization for Economic Cooperation and

Development. The OECD Observer, (268), 10-11. Retrieved April 5, 2010, from ABI/INFORM

Global. (Document ID: 1529878201).

Tucker, P. (2007). Antlike Robots. The Futurist, 41(2), 6. Retrieved on February 9, 2011 from

http://search.proquest.com.ezproxy.apollolibrary.com/docview/218576169/fulltext/12D7

6BB7C2E73260224/44?accountid=35812.

Voas, R. (2004). Technological developments open new opportunities to reduce the recidivism of convicted

drinking drivers. In: Front Lines: Linking Alcohol Services Research and Practice. Washington,

DC: NIAAA, September 2004. p. 6.

Wagner, C. & Cornish, E. (2011). Emerging Careers and How to Create Them. The Futurist. 45(1), 30-33.

Retrieved on February 9, 2011 from

http://search.proquest.com.ezproxy.apollolibrary.com/docview/811085877/fulltext/12D7

2AA6DB06D5F4479/3?accountid=35812.

Weinrath, M. (1997). The ignition interlock program for drunk drivers: A multivariate test, Crime and

Delinquency, 43-57.

Weisner, C., Matzger, H., Tam, T., & Schmidt, L. (2002). Who goes to alcohol and drug treatment?

Understanding utilization within the context of insurance. Journal of Studies on Alcohol 63:673-

682, 2002. PMID: 12529067.

Venkat, R. (2010). Competing through co-creation: innovation at two companies. Strategy &

Leadership, 38(2), 22-29. Retrieved July 12, 2010, from ABI/INFORM Global. (Document

ID: 1973490141).

Wells-Parker, E. (2004). Effectiveness of court-mandated remedial interventions for DUI offenders. In: Front

Lines: Linking Alcohol Services Research and Practice. Washington, DC: NIAAA, p. 5.

Wells-Parker, E., & Williams, M. (2004). Interpreting research for practice: A challenge for evidence-based

assessment and intervention with DWI offenders. Book reviews of Assessment and Treatment

of the DWI Offender by A. Cavaiola and C. Wuth. Contemporary Psychology: APA Review of

Books 49:161-164, 2004.

Wing, S. A review of practice and research on alcohol-impaired driving. In: Front Lines: Linking Alcohol

Services Research and Practice. Washington, DC: NIAAA. p. 8.

Photos of Charie Ann Billiot, Chrissie Ann Billiot, and Brian James Lafontaine are shown below. Some of the photos are taken by Charie Ann Billiot and Chrissie Ann Billiot's biological father, Charles Joseph Billiot, Jr. (Chuck Billiot's Photography, http://www.chuckbilliot.com).

By: Tina Schaneville

C 2012 Tina Schaneville

Photo from left to right: Brian James Lafontaine, Charie Ann Billiot,

and Chrissie Ann Billiot in October 1993 when they were 5, 4, and 3 years old.

C 2012 Tina Schaneville   Brian James Lafontaine 2005

Brian James Lafontaine (male on right, 17 yrs. old) after Prom night at Andrew

Jackson High School in Chalmette, Louisiana. A son to be proud of! – Love, Mom Tina :*

Charie Ann Billiot's last photo at 16 years old. C 2012 Chuck Billiot Photography

You will always be beautiful inside and out to me,

my lovely, Charie! – Love, Mom Tina :*

By: Tina Schaneville

Chrissie 17 yrs. old, 2007   C 2012 Chuck Billiot Photography

Chrissie Ann Billiot, my beautiful, intelligent daughter,
I love you! - Love, Mom Tina : *

Brian 3 yrs. old, 1990   C 2012 Tina Schaneville

Brian James Lafontaine, you will always be my

handsome, intelligent, and sweet little boy! - Love, Mom Tina : *

Charie 3 yrs.old, 1992   C 2012 Tina Schaneville

Charie Ann Billiot, you will always be my

beautiful, intelligent girl and doll! – Love, Mom Tina : *

C 2012 Tina Schaneville

Chrissie, my beautiful, intelligent, and sweet girl,

I love you! – Love, Mom Tina :*